Dear Parent:
Your child's love of readii

D0175802

Every child learns to read in a different way and at his or her own speed. You can help your young reader improve and become more confident by encouraging his or her own interests and abilities. You can also guide your child's spiritual development by reading stories with biblical values and Bible stories, like I Can Read! books published by Zonderkidz. From books your child reads with you to the first books he or she reads alone, there are I Can Read! books for every stage of reading:

SHARED READING
Basic language, word repetition, and whimsical illustrations, ideal for sharing with your emergent reader.

BEGINNING READING
Short sentences, familiar words, and simple concepts for children eager to read on their own.

READING WITH HELP
Engaging stories, longer sentences, and language play for developing readers.

READING ALONE
Complex plots, challenging vocabulary, and high-interest topics for the independent reader.

ADVANCED READING
Short paragraphs, chapters, and exciting themes for the perfect bridge to chapter books.

I Can Read! books have introduced children to the joy of reading since 1957. Featuring award-winning authors and illustrators and a fabulous cast of beloved characters, I Can Read! books set the standard for beginning readers.

A lifetime of discovery begins with the magical words **"I Can Read!"**

Visit www.icanread.com for information on enriching your child's reading experience.
Visit www.zonderkidz.com for more Zonderkidz I Can Read! titles.

Love your neighbor as yourself.
—*Luke 10:27*

ZONDERKIDZ

The Good Samaritan
Copyright © 2015 by Zondervan
Illustrations © 2015 by David Miles

Requests for information should be addressed to:
Zonderkidz, 3900 Sparks Drive SE, Grand Rapids, Michigan 49546

ISBN 978-0-31074662-1

All Scripture quotations, unless otherwise indicated, are taken from The Holy Bible, *New International Version®, NIV®.* Copyright © 1973, 1978, 1984, 2011 by Biblica, Inc.® Used by permission. All rights reserved worldwide.

Any Internet addresses (websites, blogs, etc.) and telephone numbers in this book are offered as a resource. They are not intended in any way to be or imply an endorsement by Zondervan, nor does Zondervan vouch for the content of these sites and numbers for the life of this book.

All rights reserved. No part of this publication may be reproduced, stored in a retrieval system, or transmitted in any form or by any means—electronic, mechanical, photocopy, recording, or any other—except for brief quotations in printed reviews, without the prior permission of the publisher.

Zonderkidz is a trademark of Zondervan.

Editor: Mary Hassinger
Art direction and design: Kris Nelson

Printed in China

15 16 17 18 19 20 /DSC / 21 20 19 18 17 16 15 14 13 12 11 10 9 8 7 6 5 4 3 2 1

Adventure BIBLE

The Good Samaritan

Pictures by David Miles

ZONDERkidz

Jesus loved to be with people.

He wanted to teach others

about his Father's love.

And people went to hear his message.

One day, a very smart man

was listening to Jesus teach.

He wanted to test Jesus.

The man asked, "Teacher,

what can I do to make sure

I have eternal life?"

Jesus smiled. He said, "What does the Law say about eternal life with the Father?"

The smart man knew this answer.

He said for all to hear,

"Love the Lord your God with all
your heart and all your soul.
Love him with all your strength
and all your mind."

The man continued, "The Law says to love your neighbor as you love yourself."

"You know the Law well.

Now go and live this way,"

said Jesus.

"Then you will have eternal life."

But the man was not done testing
how much Jesus knew about God.
He asked Jesus one more question.
"Teacher, who is my neighbor?"

The crowd became quiet.

They wanted to hear Jesus' answer.

Then Jesus told a story.

Jesus said,

"One day, there was a Jewish man

traveling to Jericho.

It was a long walk,

and he was all alone."

"Suddenly, three men jumped out.

They hurt the man

and stole everything he had,

even his clothes!

Then they ran away.

The man lay in the dirt
at the side of the road.
He could not walk,
and he could hardly talk.

A priest was walking

down the same road.

He saw the man lying in the dirt.

The priest said, "Oh, dear!

I wish I could help,

but that man is so dirty!

I can't touch him.

I want to stay clean."

The priest crossed the road
and kept walking.

He shook his head and said,
"Someone else will help him."

After a little while,

another man passed by.

This man was a helper in the temple.

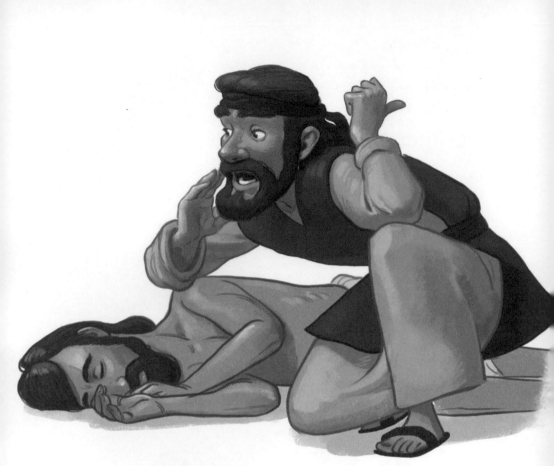

The temple helper saw the hurt man.

He frowned and said,

"That poor man!

Someone should help him.

But I am on my way to the temple.

I'm in a hurry."

The temple helper stepped

to the other side of the road.

He kept walking.

After a long time,
a third person passed by.
This person was a Samaritan.
Jews and Samaritans
did not get along.

The Samaritan saw the man
lying in the dirt.
He knew that the hurt man needed help.
He forgot that Jews and Samaritans
did not like each other.

The Samaritan knelt down.

He bandaged the man's wounds.

He put oil on cuts and bruises.

He gave the man something to drink.

Then the Samaritan

lifted the hurt man onto his donkey.

He led the donkey to an inn.

The Samaritan helped the man

into a bed at the inn.

He brought the man food and water.

He took good care of him.

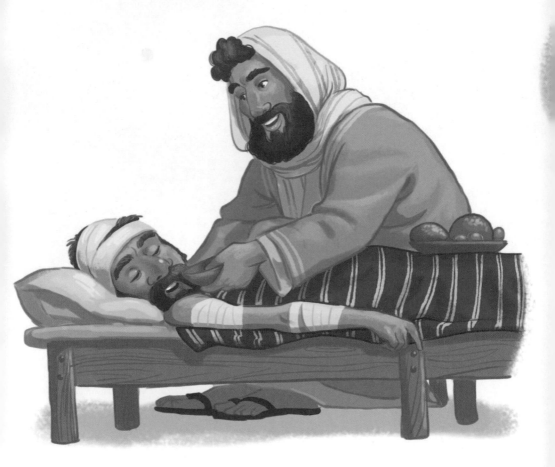

Then the Samaritan gave money

to the innkeeper.

He said, "Take care of this man.

When I come back,

I will pay you

for anything he needs."

Jesus finished his story.

He looked around at the crowd.

Then he looked at the smart man

who had asked the question.

Jesus asked the man,
"Which of the three men
who walked down the road
was a neighbor to the man
who was hurt and robbed?"

The smart man thought about it.

He said, "The man who was kind."

Jesus told the smart man,

"Go and do the same."

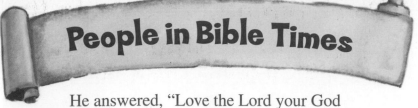

People in Bible Times

He answered, "Love the Lord your God
with all your heart and with all your strength and with all your mind
and love your neighbor as yourself."
Luke 10:27

What was a Samaritan?

A Samaritan was a person who lived in Samaria.
In Bible times, the Jews and Samaritans did not get along.
They were foreigners and did not know a lot about each other.
Jesus believed and taught that everyone should get along,
no matter what race, religion, or nationality they are.

Words to Treasure

"Which of these three do you think was a neighbor
to the man who fell into the hands of robbers?"
The expert in the law replied,
"The one who had mercy
on him."
Jesus told him, "Go and
do likewise."
Luke 10:36–37